50 Creative Sandwiches for Family Dinners

By: Kelly Johnson

Table of Contents

- Caprese Sandwich with Pesto
- Buffalo Chicken Wrap
- Mediterranean Veggie Sandwich
- BBQ Pulled Pork Sandwich
- Smoked Salmon and Cream Cheese Bagel
- Grilled Cheese with Tomato and Basil
- Cuban Sandwich
- Philly Cheesesteak
- Eggplant Parmesan Sandwich
- Turkey and Avocado Club
- Spicy Chickpea Salad Sandwich
- Banh Mi with Marinated Pork
- Reuben Sandwich
- Lobster Roll
- Italian Meatball Sub
- Pesto Chicken Sandwich
- Avocado and Bacon Toast
- French Dip Sandwich
- Falafel Wrap with Tzatziki
- Steak and Cheese Sandwich
- Tuna Salad Sandwich with Dill
- Chicken Caesar Wrap
- Shrimp Po' Boy
- Roasted Vegetable Panini
- Breakfast Sandwich with Egg and Bacon
- Vegetable Hummus Sandwich
- Crispy Chicken Sandwich
- Muffuletta Sandwich
- Tandoori Chicken Wrap
- Crispy Egg Sandwich
- Sweet Potato and Black Bean Burger
- Baked Ziti Sandwich
- Roast Beef and Horseradish Sandwich
- Cheesy Garlic Bread Sandwich
- Salami and Cheese Italian Sub

- Crispy Fish Taco Sandwich
- Pulled Jackfruit Sandwich
- Curried Chicken Salad Sandwich
- Pastrami and Swiss on Rye
- Caribbean Jerk Chicken Sandwich
- Caprese Grilled Cheese
- Corned Beef Hash Sandwich
- Savory Waffle Sandwich
- Chickpea and Avocado Smash Sandwich
- Meatloaf Sandwich with Ketchup Glaze
- Buffalo Cauliflower Sandwich
- Black Bean and Quinoa Burger
- Tropical Chicken Sandwich with Pineapple
- Zucchini Fritter Sandwich
- Apple and Cheddar Grilled Cheese

Caprese Sandwich with Pesto

Ingredients:

- 1 ciabatta roll
- 1 medium tomato, sliced
- Fresh mozzarella, sliced
- Fresh basil leaves
- 2 tablespoons pesto
- Balsamic glaze (optional)
- Salt and pepper, to taste

Instructions:

1. Slice the ciabatta roll in half and spread pesto on both halves.
2. Layer with tomato slices, mozzarella, and fresh basil leaves.
3. Drizzle with balsamic glaze, if desired, and season with salt and pepper.
4. Close the sandwich and serve immediately.

Buffalo Chicken Wrap

Ingredients:

- 1 large tortilla
- 1 cup cooked chicken, shredded
- 1/4 cup buffalo sauce
- 1/2 cup lettuce, shredded
- 1/4 cup blue cheese, crumbled
- 1/4 cup ranch dressing

Instructions:

1. In a bowl, mix shredded chicken with buffalo sauce until coated.
2. Place the tortilla on a flat surface and layer with buffalo chicken, lettuce, blue cheese, and ranch dressing.
3. Roll the tortilla tightly, slice in half, and serve.

Mediterranean Veggie Sandwich

Ingredients:

- 1 whole grain bread
- 1/4 cup hummus
- 1/4 cup feta cheese, crumbled
- Sliced cucumber
- Sliced bell peppers
- Sliced red onion
- Arugula or spinach
- Olive oil and lemon juice (for drizzling)

Instructions:

1. Spread hummus on one slice of bread.
2. Layer with feta cheese, cucumber, bell peppers, red onion, and arugula.
3. Drizzle with olive oil and lemon juice.
4. Top with the second slice of bread, slice, and serve.

BBQ Pulled Pork Sandwich

Ingredients:

- 1 cup pulled pork
- 1/4 cup BBQ sauce
- 1 hamburger bun
- Coleslaw (optional)

Instructions:

1. In a saucepan, heat pulled pork with BBQ sauce until warm.
2. Place the mixture on the hamburger bun.
3. Top with coleslaw, if desired, and serve.

Smoked Salmon and Cream Cheese Bagel

Ingredients:

- 1 bagel, sliced
- 2 oz cream cheese
- 4 oz smoked salmon
- Sliced red onion
- Capers
- Fresh dill (optional)

Instructions:

1. Spread cream cheese on both halves of the bagel.
2. Layer smoked salmon, red onion, and capers on the bottom half.
3. Top with the other half of the bagel and serve.

Grilled Cheese with Tomato and Basil

Ingredients:

- 2 slices of bread
- 2 slices of cheese (cheddar or your choice)
- 1 medium tomato, sliced
- Fresh basil leaves
- Butter

Instructions:

1. Butter one side of each slice of bread.
2. On the unbuttered side of one slice, layer cheese, tomato slices, and basil leaves.
3. Top with the second slice, buttered side out.
4. Grill in a skillet over medium heat until golden brown on both sides and cheese is melted.

Cuban Sandwich

Ingredients:

- 1 Cuban bread or sub roll
- 1/4 cup mustard
- 2 oz sliced roast pork
- 2 oz sliced ham
- 2 oz Swiss cheese
- Pickles, sliced

Instructions:

1. Slice the Cuban bread and spread mustard on both sides.
2. Layer with roast pork, ham, Swiss cheese, and pickles.
3. Close the sandwich and press in a panini press or grill until crispy and cheese melts.

Philly Cheesesteak

Ingredients:

- 1 hoagie roll
- 1/2 lb ribeye steak, thinly sliced
- 1/2 onion, sliced
- 1/2 bell pepper, sliced
- 2 slices provolone cheese
- Salt and pepper, to taste
- Olive oil

Instructions:

1. In a skillet, heat olive oil over medium heat.
2. Add sliced onion and bell pepper, sautéing until softened.
3. Add thinly sliced steak, cooking until browned and seasoned with salt and pepper.
4. Place provolone cheese on top to melt.
5. Serve in the hoagie roll.

Eggplant Parmesan Sandwich

Ingredients:

- 1 large eggplant, sliced
- 1 cup breadcrumbs
- 1 cup marinara sauce
- 1 cup mozzarella cheese, shredded
- 1/4 cup Parmesan cheese, grated
- Olive oil
- 2 sandwich rolls

Instructions:

1. Preheat the oven to 375°F (190°C).
2. Dip eggplant slices in olive oil, then coat with breadcrumbs.
3. Arrange on a baking sheet and bake for 25 minutes, flipping halfway.
4. In a sandwich roll, layer baked eggplant, marinara sauce, and mozzarella cheese.
5. Sprinkle with Parmesan and bake until cheese is melted, about 10 minutes.

Turkey and Avocado Club

Ingredients:

- 3 slices of bread (whole grain or white)
- 1/4 lb sliced turkey
- 1/2 avocado, mashed
- 2 slices bacon, cooked
- Lettuce leaves
- Tomato slices
- Mayonnaise

Instructions:

1. Toast the bread slices.
2. Spread mayonnaise on one side of each slice.
3. Layer turkey, avocado, bacon, lettuce, and tomato between two slices.
4. Top with the third slice of bread, cut in half, and serve.

Spicy Chickpea Salad Sandwich

Ingredients:

- 1 can chickpeas, drained and rinsed
- 2 tablespoons mayonnaise
- 1 tablespoon sriracha
- 1 celery stalk, diced
- Salt and pepper, to taste
- 2 slices of bread or a roll

Instructions:

1. In a bowl, mash chickpeas with a fork.
2. Stir in mayonnaise, sriracha, diced celery, salt, and pepper.
3. Spread the mixture on bread or a roll and serve.

Banh Mi with Marinated Pork

Ingredients:

- 1 baguette
- 1/2 lb pork tenderloin, marinated in soy sauce, garlic, and sugar
- Pickled carrots and daikon
- Cucumber slices
- Fresh cilantro
- Jalapeño slices (optional)
- Mayonnaise

Instructions:

1. Grill or pan-sear the marinated pork until cooked through.
2. Slice the baguette and spread mayonnaise inside.
3. Layer sliced pork, pickled vegetables, cucumber, cilantro, and jalapeños.
4. Close the baguette and serve.

Reuben Sandwich

Ingredients:

- 2 slices of rye bread
- 1/4 lb corned beef, sliced
- 2 slices Swiss cheese
- 1/4 cup sauerkraut, drained
- 2 tablespoons Russian or Thousand Island dressing
- Butter

Instructions:

1. Heat a skillet over medium heat.
2. Butter one side of each slice of bread.
3. Assemble the sandwich with corned beef, Swiss cheese, sauerkraut, and dressing between the unbuttered sides.
4. Grill in the skillet until golden brown and cheese melts, about 4-5 minutes per side.

Lobster Roll

Ingredients:

- 1 cup cooked lobster meat, chopped
- 2 tablespoons mayonnaise
- 1 tablespoon lemon juice
- 1 tablespoon celery, diced
- Salt and pepper, to taste
- 1 hot dog bun or split-top roll

Instructions:

1. In a bowl, mix lobster meat, mayonnaise, lemon juice, celery, salt, and pepper.
2. Toast the bun lightly.
3. Fill the bun with lobster mixture and serve.

Italian Meatball Sub

Ingredients:

- 1 hoagie roll
- 4-5 meatballs (homemade or store-bought)
- 1/2 cup marinara sauce
- 1/4 cup mozzarella cheese, shredded
- Fresh basil leaves (optional)

Instructions:

1. Heat the meatballs in marinara sauce.
2. Place the meatballs in the hoagie roll.
3. Top with marinara sauce and mozzarella cheese.
4. Broil until cheese is melted, and garnish with basil, if desired.

Pesto Chicken Sandwich

Ingredients:

- 1 chicken breast, grilled and sliced
- 2 tablespoons pesto
- 1 slice provolone cheese
- 1 ciabatta roll or sandwich bread
- Lettuce and tomato slices

Instructions:

1. Spread pesto on the ciabatta roll or bread.
2. Layer with grilled chicken, provolone cheese, lettuce, and tomato.
3. Close the sandwich and serve.

Avocado and Bacon Toast

Ingredients:

- 2 slices of bread (whole grain or sourdough)
- 1 ripe avocado
- 4 slices of cooked bacon
- Salt and pepper, to taste
- Red pepper flakes (optional)

Instructions:

1. Toast the bread slices until golden brown.
2. Mash the avocado in a bowl and season with salt and pepper.
3. Spread the avocado on each slice of toast.
4. Top with crispy bacon and sprinkle with red pepper flakes if desired.

French Dip Sandwich

Ingredients:

- 1 baguette or hoagie roll
- 1/2 lb thinly sliced roast beef
- 1 cup beef broth
- 1/2 cup Swiss cheese, shredded
- 1 tablespoon horseradish sauce (optional)
- Au jus for dipping

Instructions:

1. Preheat the oven to 350°F (175°C).
2. Heat the beef broth in a saucepan.
3. Slice the baguette and layer roast beef inside.
4. Top with Swiss cheese and place in the oven until cheese is melted, about 5-7 minutes.
5. Serve with heated broth for dipping.

Falafel Wrap with Tzatziki

Ingredients:

- 1 cup falafel balls, cooked
- 1 large tortilla or pita bread
- 1/2 cup lettuce, shredded
- 1/4 cup tomatoes, diced
- 1/4 cup cucumber, sliced
- 1/4 cup tzatziki sauce

Instructions:

1. Place falafel balls in the center of the tortilla or pita.
2. Top with lettuce, tomatoes, cucumber, and tzatziki sauce.
3. Roll up the wrap tightly and slice in half to serve.

Steak and Cheese Sandwich

Ingredients:

- 1 hoagie roll
- 1/2 lb ribeye steak, thinly sliced
- 1/2 onion, sautéed
- 1/2 bell pepper, sautéed
- 1/2 cup provolone cheese, shredded
- Salt and pepper, to taste

Instructions:

1. Cook the steak in a skillet over medium-high heat, seasoning with salt and pepper.
2. Add sautéed onions and bell peppers to the skillet until heated through.
3. Fill the hoagie roll with the steak mixture and top with provolone cheese.
4. Broil until the cheese melts and serve.

Tuna Salad Sandwich with Dill

Ingredients:

- 1 can tuna, drained
- 2 tablespoons mayonnaise
- 1 tablespoon Dijon mustard
- 1 tablespoon fresh dill, chopped
- Salt and pepper, to taste
- 2 slices of bread or a roll

Instructions:

1. In a bowl, mix tuna, mayonnaise, mustard, dill, salt, and pepper.
2. Spread the tuna salad on one slice of bread.
3. Top with the second slice and cut in half to serve.

Chicken Caesar Wrap

Ingredients:

- 1 large tortilla
- 1 cup cooked chicken breast, sliced
- 1/2 cup romaine lettuce, chopped
- 2 tablespoons Caesar dressing
- 2 tablespoons Parmesan cheese, grated

Instructions:

1. In a bowl, toss chicken with Caesar dressing, lettuce, and Parmesan cheese.
2. Place the mixture in the center of the tortilla.
3. Roll tightly and slice in half to serve.

Shrimp Po' Boy

Ingredients:

- 1 hoagie roll
- 1/2 lb shrimp, peeled and deveined
- 1/4 cup flour
- 1/4 cup cornmeal
- 1 tablespoon Cajun seasoning
- Lettuce and tomato slices
- Remoulade sauce

Instructions:

1. In a bowl, mix flour, cornmeal, and Cajun seasoning.
2. Dredge shrimp in the mixture and fry until golden brown.
3. Fill the hoagie roll with shrimp, lettuce, tomato, and drizzle with remoulade sauce.

Roasted Vegetable Panini

Ingredients:

- 2 slices of ciabatta or focaccia bread
- 1/2 cup mixed roasted vegetables (bell peppers, zucchini, eggplant)
- 1/4 cup mozzarella cheese, shredded
- 1 tablespoon pesto

Instructions:

1. Spread pesto on one side of each slice of bread.
2. Layer roasted vegetables and mozzarella cheese on one slice.
3. Top with the other slice of bread and grill in a panini press until crispy and cheese is melted.

Breakfast Sandwich with Egg and Bacon

Ingredients:

- 1 English muffin, split
- 1 large egg
- 2 slices of bacon
- 1 slice of cheddar cheese
- Salt and pepper, to taste

Instructions:

1. Cook bacon in a skillet until crispy, then remove and set aside.
2. In the same skillet, crack the egg and cook to your desired doneness, seasoning with salt and pepper.
3. Toast the English muffin.
4. Assemble the sandwich by placing the egg and bacon on one half of the muffin, topping with cheese, and closing with the other half.

Vegetable Hummus Sandwich

Ingredients:

- 2 slices of whole grain bread
- 1/2 cup hummus
- 1/4 cucumber, sliced
- 1/4 bell pepper, sliced
- Handful of spinach
- Salt and pepper, to taste

Instructions:

1. Spread hummus on both slices of bread.
2. Layer cucumber, bell pepper, and spinach on one slice.
3. Season with salt and pepper, then top with the other slice and cut in half.

Crispy Chicken Sandwich

Ingredients:

- 1 boneless chicken breast
- 1/2 cup flour
- 1 egg, beaten
- 1/2 cup breadcrumbs
- 1 hamburger bun
- Lettuce and tomato
- Mayonnaise

Instructions:

1. Preheat oil in a skillet for frying.
2. Dredge chicken in flour, dip in egg, then coat with breadcrumbs.
3. Fry chicken until golden brown and cooked through.
4. Assemble the sandwich with chicken, lettuce, tomato, and mayonnaise on the bun.

Muffuletta Sandwich

Ingredients:

- 1 round loaf of Italian bread
- 1/4 cup olive salad (chopped olives, peppers, garlic)
- 4 ounces sliced mortadella
- 4 ounces sliced salami
- 4 ounces sliced provolone cheese
- 2 ounces sliced ham

Instructions:

1. Slice the Italian bread in half horizontally.
2. Spread olive salad on both halves.
3. Layer mortadella, salami, provolone, and ham on the bottom half.
4. Top with the other half of the bread, press down gently, and cut into wedges.

Tandoori Chicken Wrap

Ingredients:

- 1 large tortilla
- 1 cup cooked tandoori chicken, sliced
- 1/2 cup lettuce, shredded
- 1/4 cup cucumber, sliced
- 2 tablespoons yogurt sauce

Instructions:

1. Lay the tortilla flat and layer with tandoori chicken, lettuce, cucumber, and yogurt sauce.
2. Roll the tortilla tightly, folding in the sides as you go.
3. Slice in half to serve.

Crispy Egg Sandwich

Ingredients:

- 1 large egg
- 1 tablespoon flour
- 1/4 cup breadcrumbs
- 1 hamburger bun
- Lettuce and ketchup

Instructions:

1. Dredge the egg in flour, dip in beaten egg, then coat with breadcrumbs.
2. Fry the egg until crispy and cooked through.
3. Assemble the sandwich with the crispy egg, lettuce, and ketchup on the bun.

Sweet Potato and Black Bean Burger

Ingredients:

- 1 cup cooked sweet potato, mashed
- 1/2 cup black beans, drained and mashed
- 1/2 cup breadcrumbs
- 1/4 teaspoon cumin
- Salt and pepper, to taste
- 1 hamburger bun

Instructions:

1. In a bowl, mix mashed sweet potato, black beans, breadcrumbs, cumin, salt, and pepper.
2. Form into a patty and cook in a skillet until heated through.
3. Serve on a hamburger bun with desired toppings.

Baked Ziti Sandwich

Ingredients:

- 1 hoagie roll
- 1 cup cooked ziti pasta
- 1/2 cup marinara sauce
- 1/4 cup ricotta cheese
- 1/4 cup mozzarella cheese, shredded

Instructions:

1. Preheat the oven to 350°F (175°C).
2. In a bowl, mix cooked ziti with marinara and ricotta cheese.
3. Fill the hoagie roll with the ziti mixture, top with mozzarella, and bake until the cheese is melted, about 10 minutes.

Roast Beef and Horseradish Sandwich

Ingredients:

- 2 slices of rye bread
- 4 ounces roast beef, sliced
- 1 tablespoon horseradish sauce
- 1 slice Swiss cheese
- Lettuce leaves

Instructions:

1. Spread horseradish sauce on one slice of rye bread.
2. Layer roast beef, Swiss cheese, and lettuce on top.
3. Top with the second slice of bread, cut in half, and serve.

Cheesy Garlic Bread Sandwich

Ingredients:

- 2 slices of garlic bread
- 2 slices of mozzarella cheese
- 1/4 cup marinara sauce

Instructions:

1. Preheat the oven to 400°F (200°C).
2. Place one slice of garlic bread on a baking sheet, top with mozzarella cheese, and the second slice of garlic bread.
3. Bake for 10-12 minutes until cheese is melted.
4. Serve with marinara sauce for dipping.

Salami and Cheese Italian Sub

Ingredients:

- 1 Italian sub roll
- 4 ounces salami, sliced
- 4 ounces provolone cheese, sliced
- Lettuce, tomato, and onion slices
- Italian dressing

Instructions:

1. Slice the Italian sub roll lengthwise.
2. Layer salami and provolone on one side, followed by lettuce, tomato, and onion.
3. Drizzle with Italian dressing, close the sandwich, and slice in half.

Crispy Fish Taco Sandwich

Ingredients:

- 2 corn tortillas
- 1 piece of breaded fish fillet, cooked
- Cabbage slaw
- 1/4 avocado, sliced
- Lime wedges

Instructions:

1. Warm the corn tortillas in a skillet.
2. Place the cooked fish fillet on the tortillas.
3. Top with cabbage slaw and avocado slices.
4. Serve with lime wedges on the side.

Pulled Jackfruit Sandwich

Ingredients:

- 1 hamburger bun
- 1 cup canned young jackfruit, drained and shredded
- 1/2 cup BBQ sauce
- Pickles, for topping

Instructions:

1. In a skillet, combine shredded jackfruit and BBQ sauce, cooking until heated through.
2. Serve the pulled jackfruit on a hamburger bun, topped with pickles.

Curried Chicken Salad Sandwich

Ingredients:

- 1 cup cooked chicken, shredded
- 1/4 cup mayonnaise
- 1 tablespoon curry powder
- 1/4 cup celery, chopped
- 2 slices of bread

Instructions:

1. In a bowl, mix shredded chicken, mayonnaise, curry powder, and celery.
2. Spread the chicken salad on one slice of bread, top with the second slice, and cut in half.

Pastrami and Swiss on Rye

Ingredients:

- 2 slices of rye bread
- 4 ounces pastrami, sliced
- 1 slice Swiss cheese
- Mustard, to taste

Instructions:

1. Spread mustard on one slice of rye bread.
2. Layer pastrami and Swiss cheese on top.
3. Top with the second slice of bread, slice in half, and serve.

Caribbean Jerk Chicken Sandwich

Ingredients:

- 1 chicken breast, grilled and sliced
- 1 hamburger bun
- Jerk seasoning, to taste
- Lettuce, tomato, and mango salsa

Instructions:

1. Season the grilled chicken breast with jerk seasoning.
2. Serve on a hamburger bun with lettuce, tomato, and mango salsa.

Caprese Grilled Cheese

Ingredients:

- 2 slices of sourdough bread
- 1 ball of fresh mozzarella, sliced
- 1 tomato, sliced
- Fresh basil leaves
- Balsamic glaze (optional)
- Butter, for grilling

Instructions:

1. Heat a skillet over medium heat and butter one side of each slice of bread.
2. Layer mozzarella, tomato, and basil on the unbuttered side of one slice. Drizzle with balsamic glaze if desired.
3. Top with the other slice, buttered side up.
4. Grill for about 3-4 minutes per side until golden brown and cheese is melted.

Corned Beef Hash Sandwich

Ingredients:

- 2 slices of rye bread
- 1 cup corned beef hash
- 1 egg (fried or poached)
- Mustard, to taste

Instructions:

1. Heat the corned beef hash in a skillet until crispy.
2. Place the hash on one slice of rye bread.
3. Top with the fried egg and mustard, then close with the second slice of bread.

Savory Waffle Sandwich

Ingredients:

- 2 savory waffles (made with cheese and herbs)
- 2 slices of ham or turkey
- 1/4 cup spinach or arugula
- 1 slice of cheese (like cheddar or gouda)

Instructions:

1. Toast the savory waffles until golden brown.
2. Layer ham or turkey, spinach, and cheese between the waffles.
3. Serve warm, pressing slightly to melt the cheese.

Chickpea and Avocado Smash Sandwich

Ingredients:

- 1 ripe avocado
- 1 cup canned chickpeas, drained
- 1 tablespoon lemon juice
- Salt and pepper, to taste
- 2 slices of whole-grain bread
- Lettuce or spinach

Instructions:

1. In a bowl, mash the avocado and chickpeas together with lemon juice, salt, and pepper.
2. Spread the mixture on one slice of bread, top with lettuce, and close with the second slice.

Meatloaf Sandwich with Ketchup Glaze

Ingredients:

- 2 slices of bread (white or whole grain)
- 1 slice of meatloaf (cooked)
- 1 tablespoon ketchup
- 1 slice of cheese (optional)

Instructions:

1. Spread ketchup on one side of the meatloaf.
2. Place meatloaf on one slice of bread, add cheese if desired, and top with the second slice.
3. Heat in a skillet until the sandwich is warmed through.

Buffalo Cauliflower Sandwich

Ingredients:

- 1 cup cauliflower florets, roasted
- 1/4 cup buffalo sauce
- 2 slices of bread (your choice)
- Lettuce or cabbage for crunch
- Ranch or blue cheese dressing (optional)

Instructions:

1. Toss roasted cauliflower in buffalo sauce.
2. Layer cauliflower on one slice of bread, top with lettuce, and drizzle with ranch or blue cheese dressing if desired.
3. Close with the second slice of bread.

Black Bean and Quinoa Burger

Ingredients:

- 1 black bean and quinoa burger patty (store-bought or homemade)
- 1 hamburger bun
- Lettuce, tomato, and onion for toppings
- Avocado or mayo (optional)

Instructions:

1. Cook the black bean and quinoa burger according to package instructions or your recipe.
2. Assemble the burger on a bun with your choice of toppings and condiments.

Tropical Chicken Sandwich with Pineapple

Ingredients:

- 1 grilled chicken breast
- 1 slice of pineapple, grilled
- 1 hamburger bun
- Lettuce and teriyaki sauce

Instructions:

1. Grill the chicken breast and pineapple slice.
2. Place the chicken and grilled pineapple on the bun, top with lettuce and drizzle with teriyaki sauce.

Zucchini Fritter Sandwich

Ingredients:

- 2 medium zucchinis, grated
- 1/2 cup all-purpose flour
- 1/4 cup grated Parmesan cheese
- 1 egg, beaten
- 1 teaspoon garlic powder
- Salt and pepper, to taste
- 4 slices of bread (your choice)
- Lettuce or spinach
- Tzatziki sauce or yogurt, for serving

Instructions:

1. In a bowl, combine grated zucchini, flour, Parmesan cheese, egg, garlic powder, salt, and pepper. Mix until well combined.
2. Heat a skillet over medium heat with a little oil. Drop spoonfuls of the zucchini mixture into the skillet, flattening them into fritters. Cook for 3-4 minutes on each side until golden brown.
3. Assemble the sandwich by placing the fritters on bread with lettuce and tzatziki sauce. Top with another slice of bread and serve.

Apple and Cheddar Grilled Cheese

Ingredients:

- 2 slices of bread (sourdough or whole grain)
- 1/2 cup sharp cheddar cheese, grated
- 1/2 apple, thinly sliced (preferably Granny Smith or your choice)
- 1 tablespoon butter

Instructions:

1. Butter one side of each slice of bread.
2. On the unbuttered side, layer the cheddar cheese and apple slices.
3. Top with the second slice of bread, buttered side up.
4. Heat a skillet over medium heat and grill the sandwich for about 3-4 minutes on each side until the bread is golden brown and the cheese is melted.